photo**word**book

Pets

Camilla Lloyd

zwijsen

bdyslexie
font

is the typeface used in this book

WAYLAND

First published in 2014 by Wayland
Copyright © Wayland 2014

Wayland
338 Euston Road
London NW1 3BH

Wayland Australia
Level 17/207 Kent Street
Sydney, NSW 2000

Editor: Elizabeth Brent
Designer: Amy McSimpson

Dewey number: 428.1-dc23

ISBN   978 0 7502 5153 2
eBook ISBN   978 0 7502 8534 6

Printed in China

10 9 8 7 6 5 4 3 2 1

Picture acknowledgements: All images, including the
cover image, courtesy of Shutterstock.com, except:
p4–5 © Lilun_Li/iStockPhoto, p7 © Jon Feingersh
Photography/SuperStock/Corbis, p11 © Graffizone/
iStockPhoto, p12 © Wildroze/iStockPhoto, p16–17
© SimplyCreativePhotography/iStockPhoto

The website addresses (URLs) included in this book were
valid at the time of going to press. However, it is possible
that contents or addresses may change following the
publication of this book. No responsibility for any such
changes can be accepted by either the author or the Publisher.

Wayland is a division of Hachette Children's Books, an
Hachette UK company.
www.hachette.co.uk

Contents

3

pets

These animals are pets.

Pets live with people in their home or garden.

5

goldfish

These are goldfish.

Goldfish only need a little
bit of fish food each day.

6

rabbit

This is a rabbit.

Pet rabbits eat rabbit food, vegetables and hay.

cat

This is a **cat**.

12

A baby cat is called a kitten.

13

guinea pig

This is a guinea pig.

Guinea pigs like to play with people.

hamster

This is a hamster.

Hamsters are awake at night and asleep during the day.

15

chicken

This is a
chicken.

Chickens can lay eggs for us to eat.

17

horse

This is a **horse**.

Pet **horses** sometimes live in stables.

tortoise

This is a **tortoise**.

Tortoises can live for more than 100 years!

Picture quiz

Can you find these things in the book?

cat

eggs

horse

rabbit

What pages are they on?

Index quiz

The index is on page 24.
Use the index to answer these questions.

1. Which page shows a **hamster**?
   When do hamsters like to sleep?

2. Which page shows a **dog**?
   What do dogs like to do every day?

3. Which pages show a **chicken**?
   What can chickens lay?

4. Which page shows a **tortoise**?
   How long can some tortoises live for?

Index

Answers

Picture quiz: The cat is on page 12. The eggs are on pages 16 & 17. The horse is on page 19. The rabbit is on page 11.

Index quiz: 1. Page 15, during the day; 2. Page 9, go for a walk; 3. Pages 16 & 17, eggs; 4. Page 21, more than 100 years.